CHALLENGING
Whodunit Puzzles

DR. QUICKSOLVE'S MINI-MYSTERIES

Jim Sukach
Illustrated by Lucy Corvino

Sterling Publishing Co., Inc.
New York

Thanks to Hannah Steinmetz and Lucy Corvino,
my partners in crime.

Library of Congress Cataloging-in-Publication Data

Sukach, Jim.
    Challenging whodunit puzzles : Dr. Quicksolve's mini-mysteries /
Jim Sukach : illustrated by Lucy Corvino.
        p.   cm.
    Includes index.
    ISBN 0-8069-9618-8
    1. Puzzles. 2. Detective and mystery stories. I. Title.
GV1507.D4S82   1998
793.73—dc21   97-18080
                                                  CIP

10 9 8 7 6 5 4 3

First paperback edition published in 1998 by
Sterling Publishing Company, Inc.
387 Park Avenue South, New York, N.Y. 10016
© 1997 by James Richard Sukach
Distributed in Canada by Sterling Publishing
℅ Canadian Manda Group, One Atlantic Avenue, Suite 105
Toronto, Ontario, Canada M6K 3E7
Distributed in Great Britain and Europe by Cassell PLC
Wellington House, 125 Strand, London WC2R 0BB, England
Distributed in Australia by Capricorn Link (Australia) Pty Ltd.
P.O. Box 6651, Baulkham Hills, Business Centre, NSW 2153, Australia
Printed in Hong Kong
All rights reserved

Sterling ISBN 0-8069-9618-8 Trade
            0-8069-9619-6 Paper

Contents

•••••••••

Dr. J.L. Quicksolve

• • • • • • • •

Dr. Jeffrey Lynn Quicksolve, professor of criminology, retired from the police force as a detective at a very young age. Now he works with various police agencies and private detectives as a consultant when he isn't teaching at the university.

He certainly knows his business, solving crimes. Many people are amazed at how he solves so many crimes so quickly. He says, "The more you know about people and the world we live in, the easier it is to solve a problem."

His son, Junior, enjoys learning too, and he solves a few mysteries himself.

Read, listen, think carefully, and you can solve these crimes too!

Murder Between Friends

•••••••••

The apartment building was an old house near the university. It had been divided into four apartments. The owner of the building, Gracious Host, lived in a large apartment downstairs. She rented out the three apartments upstairs. Dr. J.L. Quicksolve had heard the call over the police radio and arrived before the officers.

Gracious described her tenants to Dr. Quicksolve. She said Tweeter Woofer was a young "hippie type" who sometimes played her music too loudly. "I told her, one more complaint and she would be out on the street." Baby Blossom was hearing impaired, but "she reads lips." Terry Cloth was dead.

Gracious said she was sure only her three tenants were in the building when she heard the shots and discovered the body.

The hall was quiet when Dr. Quicksolve walked upstairs. The woman in the bathrobe lay against the wall, as if she were taking a nap. The three red stains told him the nap would last forever.

Dr. Quicksolve heard music in the back of the apartment and smelled burning incense when Tweeter Woofer opened her apartment door to let him enter. Miss Woofer was shocked when he explained what had happened. As they stood inside the door, she said, "This is so upsetting.

Who would shoot Terry?" She said she did not hear anything and did not see anything.

Dr. Quicksolve knocked quietly on Baby Blossom's door. She and her dog, a yellow Labrador, came to the door. He explained what happened. "I was a little afraid to open the door because I thought I heard shots," she said. "I guess I was right."

When Dr. Quicksolve went back downstairs, the policemen had arrived. "I have a good suspect," he told them.

Which woman did he suspect?

Answer on page 89.

Inheritance

· · · · · · · · ·

"A small turtle sundae, please," Dr. J.L. Quicksolve told the waitress. He was the last to order. His friend, Fred Fraudstop, had invited Dr. Quicksolve and his son, Junior, for an ice cream treat to celebrate Fred's move into town. Fred ordered a chocolate-marshmallow sundae, and Junior ordered a "freight train"—two banana splits in separate glass bowls pulled by a glass train engine. If you ate the whole thing, you got to keep the glass engine. Junior had five of them at home.

"That reminds me of a railroad tycoon who died recently. He was an only child and a bachelor who kept to himself, though he loved to travel through the West when he was younger. Studying the Old West was a hobby of his. We had to hunt for his next-of-kin," Fred said as Junior's ice cream was brought out by two waitresses wearing conductor's caps and red bandannas.

"Did you find anybody?" Junior asked, reaching for his spoon.

"They found us," Fred said, "which wasn't surprising considering the money they stood to inherit. I've narrowed it down to two people. The rest are obviously just pretending to be relatives, hoping to get the money."

"Who are they?" Junior asked.

"One is a niece from Chicago, and the other is a cousin from North Dakota. They're the only ones who don't have a previous record of fraud of some sort or another. I still have to check out their claims, though. Would you like to talk to them with me?" he asked Dr. Quicksolve.

"Sure; it sounds interesting," the detective answered. "Let's start with the one from North Dakota."

Why did Dr. Quicksolve want to talk to the relative from North Dakota?

Answer on page 90.

Quicksolve, the Movie

• • • • • • • •

Dr. J.L. Quicksolve liked large, older theaters. They were grander than the smaller modern ones. This venerable old movie palace had huge, many-colored dragons painted on the massive walls. Dr. Quicksolve was with his son, Junior, and their friends Captain Reelumin and Sergeant Shurshot. The cloudy day and the drizzling rain outside could not begin to dampen their excitement. It was the premiere of *Quicksolve,* a film loosely based on his life as a detective. It was an early sellout. The parking lot was full, and cars lined the street for several blocks.

Just as the lights dimmed and the previews were about to begin, Dr. Quicksolve felt a tap on his shoulder. "We've been robbed, sir," the attendant said. Dr. Quicksolve and his entourage spoke with the manager immediately. As they walked toward the front door, the manager explained that someone had entered his office, struck his assistant manager over the head, and robbed them.

As they walked outside, they saw a young couple pulling out of a parking spot near the door. Captain Reelumin and Sergeant Shurshot stepped to the front of the car, raising their hands to indicate that the driver should stop. Dr. Quicksolve went to the driver's window as Sergeant Shurshot moved around cautiously to the passenger's side. "Hello," the detective said to the driver. "Did you change your mind about the movie?"

"No," the driver said nervously, obviously recognizing Dr. Quicksolve. "We just got here too late. The tickets are all sold out, so we couldn't get in."

"I don't think that's the truth," Dr. Quicksolve said.

Why doesn't Dr. Quicksolve believe him?

Answer on page 91.

Shattered Crystal

• • • • • • • •

Dr. J.L. Quicksolve felt the cool east wind on the back of his neck as he knocked on the front door. In spite of the clear morning sunshine, he felt a chill as he looked at the three splintered bullet holes in the door. Sergeant Rebekah Shurshot let the detective into the house, and Crystal Goblet explained what happened.

"I've been afraid lately. I think someone has been following me," she said. "I keep seeing a black Ford Escort in my rearview mirror."

"The Ford Escort is one of the most popular cars in America," Sergeant Shurshot interrupted. "We all see them in our rearview mirrors."

Crystal went on, "I thought my husband was at work. His secretary, Miss Laptop, called around six to tell me my husband would be working late yesterday."

"Does his secretary usually call you when your husband works late?" Sergeant Shurshot asked.

"Too usually," Crystal reflected with a note of bitterness. "So when I heard someone at the front door," she continued, "I was frightened. I thought someone was breaking in. So I got my husband's gun and I hid behind the door. When the door opened I saw a shadow fall across the floor. I knew someone had come into my house. I didn't wait to see who it was. I was too frightened. I shot through the door. When I looked around the door, I couldn't believe I saw my husband lying dead on the floor. I was shattered."

Sergeant Shurshot looked at Dr. Quicksolve and shook her head.

"No. It wasn't an accident, was it, Mrs. Goblet?" Quicksolve asked.

Why didn't they believe her story?

Answer on page 92.

Professor Wright

• • • • • • • • •

Professor William Longfellow Shakespeare Wright
was a professor of English, as had been his father
before him. Professor Wright, a good friend of Dr.
J.L. Quicksolve, was in a coma from damage
caused by a five-story fall from his office window
at the university.

"Apparently a suicide attempt," Captain Reelumin told Dr. Quicksolve as they looked out Dr.
Wright's office window down to the lawn below.
"I'm sorry. I know he was your friend. He left a
note," Reelumin said, handing the note to Quicksolve.

The note said, "I have been unfair in the way I
graded a certain student. He was unable to con-
tinue on his academic scholarship, and I am to
blame. If I were him, I would be angry enough to
kill. Fortunately, he is not like that. I am so
ashamed. I will do it myself. I hope my family and
friends will forgive me." The note was typed and
unsigned.

"You found this here in the office?" Dr. Quicksolve asked.

"Yes. It was on his desk," Captain Reelumin
said.

Dr. Quicksolve looked around the room. It was
meticulously neat. Books lined three walls from
the floor to the ceiling. A large desk was in the

center of the room. A computer screen was to the left. A thick notebook was on the right. A picture of Professor Wright's wife and children was on the desk. His father's portrait stared down from the wall.

"We need to find the student who was so upset about his final grade that he did this. We must find him before he leaves the campus for the summer break," Dr. Quicksolve said. "This was not a suicide attempt."

Why does Dr. Quicksolve think someone tried to murder Professor Wright?

Answer on page 93.

Strikeout

· · · · · · · · ·

Dr. J.L. Quicksolve and Junior were meeting Fred Fraudstop for lunch. Fred said he had to stop and question a man about a burglary at the Strikeout Sportscard Shop. Dr. Quicksolve decided to go with him because Junior was a baseball card collector and would be interested in the shop, not to mention Quicksolve's curiosity about the burglary.

"We were broken into overnight," Homer Hitter, the shop owner, told them. "They took a bunch of cards, but mostly money," he said, showing them the back door that had been jimmied open and the empty moneybox. "We close late, so I usually take the money to the bank in the morning," he said.

"Did you lock up last night?" Dr. Quicksolve asked him. Junior was looking at a display of Mickey Mantle cards. He showed his dad the 1953 rookie card that had a price of $300 on it. "Save your money," Dr. Quicksolve said.

"No, my clerk, Art Dunn, closed up last night. He always closes up. He bolts the back door and goes out the front. I let him have his own key. I don't think he would do anything like this." Then he noticed Junior looking at the cards. "You like Mickey Mantle?" he asked Junior. He reached below the counter and brought out a card that showed Mantle standing at the left side of the plate as if he were waiting for a pitch. "Without all those injuries he would have been the Home Run King."

"What do you think of the Strikeout Sportscard Shop?" Fred asked Junior as they walked out onto the sidewalk.

"I don't think I'd buy anything from that guy," Junior said, "and you probably should doubt what he tells you about the robbery."

Why does Junior mistrust Homer?

Answer on page 94.

Coddled Coed

● ● ● ● ● ● ● ●

Three college coeds rented the house next to Dr. J.L. Quicksolve. Brenda Broadcloth and Cherry Ripple, two of them, ran up to Dr. Quicksolve in front of his house just as he was saying goodbye to Sergeant Rebekah Shurshot. Brenda said they had been robbed.

The three roommates had shopped together. They had bought their groceries, including cod for that night's dinner because Holly Mackeral loved fish. Brenda chose asparagus for the vegetable, and Cherry chose vanilla ice cream for dessert.

"I had the money, but I put it back in the cookie jar when we got home," Brenda said. "Then I went upstairs to call my boyfriend. That was about three o'clock."

"I fed the cat and went out to work in the backyard. I decided to get bananas for the ice cream," Cherry said, "so I went to the cookie jar for the money around four-thirty. The money was gone. I guess someone came into the house and took it."

Holly came walking up with their dog Furball on a leash. Brenda told her about the robbery. Sergeant Shurshot asked Holly what she did after they came back from shopping.

"I unwrapped the fish and put it on the counter to thaw a little. Then I went to the basement to read. Shortly after four I put the fish in the oven and took the dog for a walk. I didn't see anybody," she said.

"Will you check the cookie jar for fingerprints?" Brenda asked Sergeant Shurshot.

"I don't think that will be necessary. This was an inside job," Sergeant Shurshot responded.

What did Sergeant Shurshot mean?

Answer on page 95.

Motorcycle Getaway

•••••••••

As they drove down the highway on Dr. J.L. Quicksolve's motorcycle, Quicksolve and Junior talked to each other through the communication systems built into their helmets. Dr. Quicksolve had just told Junior he would be old enough to drive a motorcycle when he was 40.

"By Michigan law..." Junior protested.

"By my law," Dr. Quicksolve interrupted. He waved to a motorcyclist going by in the opposite direction. A few minutes later they turned into a gas station and pulled up to the pump.

Just then, a police car sped up to the door and stopped in a no-parking area. Officer Longarm jumped out and went into the station.

Dr. Quicksolve knew something was up. He knew Officer Longarm did not take advantage of his office by parking in a no-parking zone unless he had police business to deal with.

Dr. Quicksolve walked through the door. The man at the counter was describing the robber's getaway. "He raced out that door and leaped on his motorcycle from behind, like they jumped on horses in the old Westerns. He must have had the engine running, because he never hesitated for anything once he got his hands on the money. He held the money box to his chest and flew out the door and was gone," the clerk explained.

"What did he look like?" Dr. Quicksolve asked.

"He was pretty ordinary. He was about six feet tall. He wore a black leather jacket. I think he needed a shave. When he pulled that gun I was too scared to think about that stuff. I was just hoping he wouldn't shoot me!"

The clerk looked surprised when Dr. Quicksolve smiled wryly and shook his head. "Sometimes it seems as if there are more robberies than robbers," he said.

What did Dr. Quicksolve mean?

Answer on page 92.

Telephone Ring

• • • • • • • •

Dr. J.L. Quicksolve and Junior sat in the airport waiting for Captain Reelumin's plane to arrive. Junior liked to watch the people going by. He liked to guess things about who they might be and where they were going.

Dr. Quicksolve watched people make phone calls at a round table filled with telephones, each with its tiny "booth," small dividers that separated the phones. He noticed one man kept a phone to his ear with one hand. He held a pencil with the other hand, as if he was getting instructions or directions, but he had not written anything down. A man in a jacket took the phone in the adjoining booth. He took a card out of his pocket that he looked at as he spoke into the telephone.

The first man finally wrote something down.

"See those two men?" Dr. Quicksolve asked his son.

"Yes," Junior said, noticing that his father was staring at the two men by the phones. The one in the jacket walked away, and the other man suddenly hung up his phone. Then he held it to his ear again and began making another call, talking into the phone as he looked down at his notepad.

"Get that man," Dr. Quicksolve said quietly, pointing to the man in the jacket who had just walked by them. Dr. Quicksolve walked up behind the man on the telephone and looked over his shoulder.

What did he expect to see?

Answer on page 89.

Ben Boinkt

•••••••

Dr. J.L. Quicksolve walked in the open door, passed a man lying on the couch with an icepack on his head, and proceeded into the dining room, following the voices he heard.

"That's Ben Boinkt out there on the couch," Officer Longarm said to Dr. Quicksolve.

A woman sat at the table. She had so much makeup on, Dr. Quicksolve wondered what she really looked like. Then, through the doorway that led to the kitchen, he saw the body of a woman.

"Mrs. Boinkt is dead," Officer Longarm said, answering the unspoken question. "This is Miss Glenda Cheatenhart," he said, indicating the woman at the table. "She lives next door. She found the Boinkts lying on the floor in the kitchen."

Dr. Quicksolve looked into the kitchen, where the body lay. The back door lock had been broken, and the door was open.

"I heard the crash of the door in the kitchen," Mr. Boinkt said as he stood in the dining-room doorway holding the icepack to his head. Then I heard my wife falling down when the thugs hit her from behind. There were two of them. They never said a word and they wore masks. I turned to run, but they caught me from behind and knocked me out cold. They went upstairs to the wall safe in our bedroom. They took my wife's jewels and about $200 in cash."

"I saw what happened in the kitchen through my window next door," Glenda said. "I called the police right away and ran over here with my gun, but they were gone."

Dr. Quicksolve looked at Ben and Glenda. He walked up the stairs without saying a word. When he came down, he said, "I think Mr. Boinkt needs his head examined."

What did he mean?

Answer on page 90.

Socks

• • • • • • • • •

Bobby Socks looked menacing sitting in Mr. Paddlebottom's office when Junior and Kimberly Kay walked into the principal's office. Bobby wore his jeans tucked into baseball socks just below his knees. Most kids thought it looked funny. That suited Bobby fine because he used every excuse he could think of to start a fight. He had beaten up almost every boy in school at one time or another over some imagined insult. Junior was one of the few boys Bobby would not mess with, though. Junior figured Bobby was afraid to pick on the son of the famous Dr. J.L. Quicksolve. It was as if he had something to hide and was afraid Junior would figure it out. He was right.

Kimberly's new skateboard had been stolen from her garage yesterday afternoon. She was sure she had seen Bobby in his baseball uniform pushing her bike away. Mr. Paddlebottom wanted to talk to Kimberly and Bobby before he called Bobby's parents or the police. Kimberly had asked Junior to go with her to the office for moral support.

"It was seven o'clock," Kimberly said when the principal asked her the time she thought she saw Bobby taking her bike. "I was looking out the front door for my girlfriend. Her dad was going to take us shopping," she said.

"I was playing baseball in the park at seven,"

Bobby said. "We were playing those bums from Jackson. We were just getting our last bats. We were ahead five to nothing when I hit my second home run of the game. Then I walked home with Michael Thomas. You can ask him."

"You can't believe Bobby's story, Mr. Paddlebottom," Junior said to the principal.

Why doesn't Junior believe Bobby is telling the truth?

Answer on page 93.

Buz

• • • • • • • • •

"I like doing puzzles, solving mysteries, and stuff like that," Junior explained to his grandfather, Phineas Quicksolve, as they sat at the breakfast table. Junior spoke between bites, methodically shoveling away at the huge stack of pancakes Grandma Quicksolve had made for him.

"We've got a mystery," Grandpa said, "the mystery of the missing tea." He went on to explain that Grandma made sun tea that she left on an upside-down crate in the backyard each morning. About twice a week it disappeared. Grandpa suspected Buz Stinger, the boy next door, because he had seen him out in the field behind their house two or three times on days when the tea was missing.

After breakfast they went out back to check on the jar of tea Grandma had put out that morning. It was gone. "There's Buz," Grandpa said, pointing to a boy out in the field walking away from them.

Junior walked fast to catch up to the boy. He avoided running so Buz would not think he was being chased and run away. As Junior got closer he could see Buz had a jar in his hand. It was empty.

"What are you doing?" Junior asked, trying to sound friendly.

"I'm catching bees for my collection," Buz said, looking around as if searching for a little victim. "I almost got that yellow jacket," he said, indicating a large black-and-yellow-striped bee several yards out of reach.

"Do you know a lot about bees?" Junior asked.

"Oh, yes. I study them. I just need that yellow jacket and I'll have an example of all the kinds you see around here. By the way, I'm Buz Stinger. Who are you?"

"I'm Junior Quicksolve, the guy who caught you stealing my grandma's tea," Junior replied.

Why is Junior so sure Buz stole the tea?

Answer on page 94.

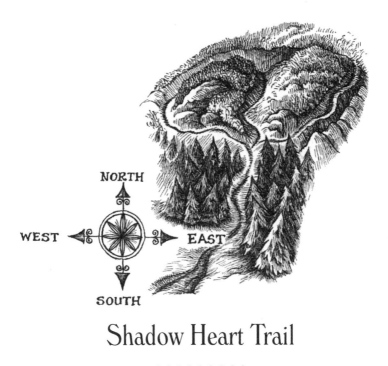

Shadow Heart Trail

• • • • • • • • •

"We'll go in small groups, leaving every 20 minutes. If you keep quiet as you hike, you'll see more wildlife," Junior's science teacher, Mr. Crucible, explained to the class as they prepared to begin their nature hike. "Remember," he said, "this is called Shadow Heart Trail because it goes north for two miles through a thick forest of pine trees and then forks left and right into the tough, rocky terrain. You can go either way, because each trail circles back and straightens out at an angle to bring you right back here. The trails make a heart shape. You can't get lost either way. Each group will have a walkie-talkie to call me if you have any problems."

Junior and his friends Shortstop, Danny Dos, and Prissy Powers were in the second group. They waited in the warmth of the early morning sun, checking their backpacks, lunches, and canteens. The first group disappeared into the woods. When about 20 minutes had passed, Junior's group headed into the woods with Mr. Crucible.

Their eyes adjusted to the shadowy darkness of the woods. They stopped to pull jackets and sweaters out of their backpacks because of the cool temperatures under the tall pines.

Suddenly there was a message on Mr. Crucible's walkie-talkie. The voice crackled weakly over the small device. "Help," it said. "We're about two and a half miles out. We climbed a hill, and the sun was bright in our eyes. Kimberly stepped off the trail and fell into a ravine. She hurt her leg badly. Please..." The voice faded away.

Mr. Crucible tried to get more information, but the walkie-talkie was not working. "Let's hurry," he said. The group began to jog through the woods.

Finally they cleared the woods, coming out into the bright sunlight and the fork in the road.

"Now which way?" Mr. Crucible asked as he looked left and right down the two trails.

"This way," Junior replied, heading to the right without hesitation.

How did Junior know which way to go?

Answer on page 93.

Thanksgiving Blessing

•••••••••

Dr. J.L. Quicksolve sat at his desk listening to his friend Divine Blessing nervously explaining her predicament and her fear of losing her inheritance.

"My mother's doctor told her it was unlikely she would ever have children," she told Dr. Quicksolve. "My father went ahead and wrote an informal will leaving everything they had to their only relative, their nephew Toby Tugfest. Then I was born, a big surprise, on Thanksgiving Day. My father recorded the event in his diary." Divine handed a copy of a page from her father's diary to Dr. Quicksolve who read an entry from 1941. "We are the proud parents of a healthy baby girl, Divine Blessing, who shall be the sole heir to all we own. Robert Blessing." Then he asked, "This is your father's signature?"

"Yes, there's no question about that. He told me he signed this page of his diary on purpose, assuming the signature would make it a legal document and serve as a will to allow me to receive my inheritance."

"And the problem?" Dr. Quicksolve asked.

"Toby Tugfest has a lawyer who claims the diary is a fake because the date is too early to be Thanksgiving Day, the fourth Thursday in November. He said that makes the original will binding and he should get my father's inheritance.

"Dr. Quicksolve, I don't know if my parents celebrated Thanksgiving Day early or if they were confused with all the excitement about having a baby or what, but this is not a fake! What can I do?"

"No, your parents were not confused," Dr. Quicksolve said gently, "and they had every right to feel especially grateful that Thanksgiving Day you were born."

What did Dr. Quicksolve mean?

Answer on page 89.

The Mysterious Woman

• • • • • • • •

The mysterious woman was a jewel thief who attended fancy parties and usually left with the jewels of the host or special guests. She was a master of disguises and rarely looked the same. She had managed to slip away time and again, and now she was back in town.

This time Lieutenant Rootumout and Dr. Quicksolve were ready for her. Dr. Quicksolve's friend Fred Fraudstop was to have a lavish party to celebrate his purchase of a spacious new home and to display his collection of fine art . Word was spread about the large and valuable collection of jewels Lucy Looker had left in his safe while she was out of town. Dr. Quicksolve, Lieutenant Rootumout, and several other police officers would be at the party.

Would she be lured by the jewels, or would she sense a trap?

Capture

●●●●●●●●●

The party was lavish, indeed. The spacious room was filled with well-dressed people talking happily and enjoying the drinks and hors d'oeuvres brought around by smiling servers.

"You both have seen her before?" Fred Fraudstop asked Dr. Quicksolve and Lieutenant Rootumout as they looked over the crowd of people.

"Yes," Dr. Quicksolve answered, "but that doesn't mean a lot. I know she looked about your height at that last party. I might recognize her walk. But remember, she's a master of disguises. She isn't likely to look like she did the last time we saw her. The best thing we can do is to look for strangers. I know most of the people you invited. Everyone else is a suspect."

"I'm going upstairs to the library, where the paintings are on display. I'm sure people will have questions," Fred said.

Dr. Quicksolve and Lieutenant Rootumout watched Fred work his way through the party crowd and climb the stairs. "See anyone suspicious?" Lieutenant Rootumout asked Dr. Quicksolve. Just then a beautiful woman began climbing the stairs across the room. Both men watched her closely until she reached the top of the stairs, where she turned to the right, out of sight. Dr. Quicksolve knew the house. There were only two

rooms in the direction she turned—the library, where the paintings were displayed, and Fred's bedroom, where the jewels were locked in his safe.

"That's her," Dr. Quicksolve said as he began to work his way through the crowd. Many people recognized him as he passed, and he had to say a few words of greeting to avoid being rude, which slowed his progress and increased his anxiety and sense of déjà vu.

He eventually reached the stairs and climbed them quickly, with Lieutenant Rootumout right behind, hand on his pistol. Looking into the bedroom, they saw the open safe.

"She didn't come downstairs," Lieutenant Rootumout said.

Dr. Quicksolve checked the windows, which they had nailed shut to prevent her escape. "Look around," he said.

"Here!" Lieutenant Rootumout picked up something from behind the door. It was a small purse, overflowing with jewels.

"She's still up here," Dr. Quicksolve said, leaving the bedroom and entering the library.

There were three people in the library quietly looking at the paintings with their backs to Dr. Quicksolve and Lieutenant Rootumout. There was Fred Fraudstop and another man an inch shorter than Fred, but with more hair. The third person was a woman a little taller than either man.

"Arrest the man," Dr. Quicksolve said.

Why the man?

Answer on page 92.

Final Payoff

• • • • • • • • •

Dr. J.L. Quicksolve and Junior had invited several of their friends who did not have families in town for Thanksgiving dinner . Dr. Quicksolve was just beginning to carve the turkey when the telephone rang. He talked briefly, then excused himself and left. Sergeant Rebekah Shurshot left with him. Junior took over the job of carving the turkey.

Three police cars were parked in the circle drive when Dr. Quicksolve and Sergeant Shurshot arrived in Dr. Quicksolve's Volkswagen Beetle that he and Junior had recently finished restoring. He pulled over to the right, parking on the grass a little to leave plenty of room for other cars to drive by.

The dead man sat crumpled over his desk. His head lay in a surprisingly small puddle of blood. A revolver lay on the desk beside him on the right. An open letter lay to his left.

"Looks like suicide," Officer Longarm said. "He is—or, should I say, was—Perry Payoff, a lobbyist. Some people say he is—er, was—one of the most powerful men in the state. He lived with a lot of pressure."

"And a lot of enemies," Sergeant Shurshot added.

Officer Longarm continued: "His wife said he was despondent over a letter he received today.

She said he walked into his office soon after he got the mail and closed the door. A few minutes later she heard the shot. She ran in and found him like this."

"The letter?" Dr. Quicksolve asked.

"The letter on his desk is from a state senator who was threatening to have him indicted for bribery and fraud. His wife said he stood to lose his job and his reputation even if the accusations were never proven."

"It looks like murder to me," Sergeant Shurshot said firmly as Perry's wife, Patti, came to the office door.

"And here's our suspect," Dr. Quicksolve added quietly.

Obviously puzzled, Officer Longarm looked at Sergeant Shurshot, Dr. Quicksolve, and finally Mrs. Payoff, whose face turned pale.

Why did Sergeant Shurshot and Dr. Quicksolve suspect Patti Payoff of killing her husband?

Answer on page 95.

Fakeout

●●●●●●●●

Sergeant Rebekah Shurshot and Officer Longarm were happy to have company for their overnight stakeout when Dr. Quicksolve asked if he could join them. They had spent another night hidden among the trees in a park on the edge of town watching a small farmhouse. A light snow fell, covering the ground and creating a beautiful scene and slippery roads. The farmhouse was the home of the girlfriend of Wallace Webb. Webb, alias Spider, was a recent escapee from State Prison. The night was as uneventful as the previous four, but at least they had the pleasure of swapping stories with the famous dectective and their good friend, Dr. J.L. Quicksolve.

They finally got something worth their attention as Sergeant Shurshot was driving Dr. Quicksolve home. A nearby party store had been robbed. The store owner did not have a good description of the robber's car, but he did know what direction it had taken. Sergeant Shurshot turned on her flashing lights and sped down the narrow country road. "There isn't likely to be anyone out here this early but the robber," she said to Dr. Quicksolve, who sat beside her.

The road was long and straight with nothing but trees on either side for miles. The sergeant slowed as they approached a car on the side of the road. The trunk was up, and a man was just pulling his jack from under the car. Sergeant Shurshot sped by as Dr. Quicksolve said, "Our first suspect."

"He was putting the jack away. He must have changed his tire already, meaning he's been there too long to be our suspect," Sergeant Shurshot explained, obviously proud of her logic. "I'll call Officer Longarm and have him check the guy out to be sure," she said, reaching for the microphone on the dashboard.

A few minutes later Officer Longarm called back over the radio. He said he was with the car on the side of the road behind them. He checked the tire in the trunk. It was flat, so the driver seemed to have a good alibi. He was surprised, though, that the man had no identification.

"I have a question about the tire," Dr. Quicksolve said.

What question? What did the detective suspect?

Answer on page 94.

Drive-By Incident

• • • • • • • •

Dr. J.L. Quicksolve waited in his car for his friend Fred Fraudstop to come out of his insurance office and join him for lunch. They were going to one of the few old-fashioned drive-in restaurants that still had waitresses and waiters who brought the orders out to the car. He dusted the dashboard of his VW Beetle as he watched a man and woman come out of Fred's office. The man wore a base-ball cap and a sweatshirt, and his arm was in a sling. The woman wore a sweatshirt and shorts. They got into a convertible, and the man drove away using his left hand to steer.

"An interesting case?" Dr. Quicksolve asked, indicating the couple leaving in the convertible as Fred got into the Beetle.

"They're suing a client of mine. They say she hit that guy's arm with her car and broke it last Friday evening. My client was driving home from work. She said she remembered passing a guy on a bike, but she doesn't think she hit him. He claims he was waving her to pass and she gunned her engine, racing by so close that she hit his arm before he could pull it back. Then she drove off. He got her license number and called the police after he had gotten home and gone to the hospital."

"Anything else unusual about the situation?" Dr. Quicksolve asked.

"No. She said she was driving the speed limit and he didn't do anything wrong, either. She never saw him wave, though. She said she just honked her horn as a warning and drove past him."

"Any witnesses?"

"No. There's no mark on her car, and the police haven't charged her. It's just her word against his. He's asking for a lot of money, but I have the feeling he'd settle for less," Fred said.

"I think he's the one who'll be charged, and he might settle for a little time in jail," Dr. Quicksolve said.

Why is the "victim" going to jail?

Answer on page 90.

Thurston Drinker

•••••••••

Dr. J.L. Quicksolve watched closely and listened intently as Thurston Drinker described his ordeal at the hands of kidnappers. Mr. Drinker appeared to be about 20 years old. He was tall and handsome with a narrow mustache. His dirty face and clothes seemed to be evidence he had, indeed, been held as a prisoner in the woods for two weeks as he claimed. He held a coffee mug with both hands, sipping frequently as he told his story.

"I was home alone when two men with ski masks charged through the front door, grabbed me, gagged me, and covered my head with some kind of sack. They dragged me into a van and drove away. We drove for an hour or two before they stopped. It was dark, but I could tell by the sounds we were in the woods."

"Did they uncover your eyes, Mr. Drinker?" asked Dr. Quicksolve.

"No. They kept my head covered except when they fed me, usually a hamburger, and no more than twice a day," Thurston replied. "Over a week went by. Apparently they had gotten ransom money from my rich uncle. Then they left and did not come back. They had kept me tied up in a tent. It took me a while to figure out they had gone, and then it took a lot of time for me to get untied. It was dark, and I realized I was lost in the woods. I wandered around for hours until I finally found some campers who took me to the police who brought me here. I am awfully tired. Can I go home now and get some food and rest?"

"Well, I don't think you can go home, but you will get plenty of food and rest," Dr. Quicksolve said.

Why did Dr. Quicksolve suspect Mr. Drinker was lying?

Answer on page 94.

Benjamin Clayborn Blowhard

· · · · · · · · · ·

Because Benjamin Clayborn Blowhard is a friend
of Sergeant Rebekah Shurshot, Dr. J.L. Quick-

solve tolerates him—barely. Dr. Quicksolve dislikes very few people. He appreciates Will Rogers' philosophy, "I've never met a man I didn't like," although he won't say that it's completely true for himself. Of course, he gets very angry at murderers of innocent people, wife-abusers, and child-molesters. He thinks that people who commit such crimes should be locked up, even though he knows that poverty, abuse, prejudice, or mental instability can lead people to do terrible things.

Dr. Quicksolve can't find any such excuse for Benjamin Clayborn Blowhard, except perhaps the mental instability part. Blowhard is not a criminal, as far as can be proven...yet. But his haughty attitude and outright lies continually upset Dr. Quicksolve.

Benjamin Clayborn Blowhard dresses the part of the great world adventurer. His cowboy hat, pinned up on one side and tied under his chin with what he says is a shark's-tooth slide, his khaki jungle jacket with loops for shotgun shells, and his alligator boots display him to the world as a man who has been there and back. He has the stories to prove he is the man he appears to be, but are his stories true?

Australian Adventure

•••••••••

Dr. J.L. Quicksolve, Sergeant Rebekah Shurshot, Junior Quicksolve, and Benjamin Clayborn Blowhard sat in a restaurant for afternoon tea. Dr. Quicksolve drank coffee, and Junior took the opportunity to have a banana split. Benjamin Clayborn Blowhard was telling stories of his adventure, danger, and daring. Junior enjoyed Blowhard's stories. To him, they were verbal cartoons. Dr. Quicksolve was trying to be pleasant, relax, and avoid a headache. Sergeant Rebekah Shurshot was fascinated.

"I was deep in the Australian Outback, alone and making camp along a rushing river, when something frightened my horse and caused him to run, abandoning me in the middle of wild and dangerous country," Blowhard said. "It didn't take long to figure out what had scared the horse. A huge bear came storming out of the brush, bent on having me for dinner and not as a guest. I dove into the river thinking the bear would not follow me into the strong current of white water. Clinging to a rock, I watched the bear pace back and forth, deciding what to do.

"Suddenly something grabbed my boot and pulled me under the foaming water. Below the surface, desperate for air, I realized a five-foot alligator was also inviting me for dinner. I pulled out my knife and struggled with the beast as the current bounced us along the rocks, pulling us downstream.

"Finally the alligator had enough, released my boot, and was swept away. I struggled to the shore. Fortunately the bear gave up too and was gone when I dragged myself back to camp, where I fell facedown into my tent and slept for three hours."

"Wow!" Sergeant Shurshot said. Junior laughed and dug into his ice cream. Dr. Quicksolve just shook his head.

What was wrong with Blowhard's story?

Answer on page 95.

Floating Above
South Dakota

· · · · · · · · ·

Just about the only time Dr. J.L. Quicksolve tried to "tune out" instead of listening intently was when Benjamin Clayborn Blowhard was giving a speech. Whenever Benjamin Clayborn Blowhard was speaking, he was giving a speech. This time, though, he was speaking about one of Dr. Quicksolve's favorite states, South Dakota, and Dr. Quicksolve felt compelled to listen.

Blowhard talked about Mount Rushmore as if he had picked the presidents to be represented and then carved them himself. Dr. Quicksolve was intrigued by stories of Wild Bill Hickok, Calamity Jane, and George Custer. Yet, the most intriguing part of Blowhard's story was how he traveled around South Dakota.

"I wanted an eagle's-eye view," he told Dr. Quicksolve and Sergeant Rebekah Shurshot. "I had friends follow me in a couple of Jeeps, of course. You always do that when you fly a hot-air balloon. But I went up alone. I like to be captain of the ship. I like to control my own destiny—like the eagle himself. I told them where I was going and when I would land. They just had to meet me and be on time.

"There's nothing like the view of Mount Rushmore from a balloon. From there I went to Rapid City, then Aberdeen. I decided to fly straight to Sioux Falls from there. I saw some of the most beautiful sights in the world up there in my balloon. I saw the Badlands, herds of buffalo, acre after acre of farmland, and highways that stretched across the country like black ribbons. You should have been there with me."

Dr. Quicksolve was in a good mood because he loved a good story. He chuckled quietly and refused to comment about the ridiculousness of Blowhard's claims.

What was so ridiculous?

Answer on page 90.

The Real McCoy

• • • • • • • •

The men were in the den sipping coffee or root beer. Dr. J.L. Quicksolve had invited several friends for dinner. Since Benjamin Clayborn Blowhard was making his nest on Sergeant Rebekah Shurshot's couch for the week, he was also invited. As usual, Blowhard was doing the talking—this time about his ancestors.

"The men on my father's side were nomadic adventurers like I am," he said. He had spoken of that side of his family before. According to him, his family spread across the globe, meeting and aiding, instructing, or encouraging more famous people than are found in a series of John Jakes novels.

"My mother's side was a little more stable," he went on, "living and prospering in the beautiful state of Virginia. Their name was McCoy. In fact, the expression 'the real McCoy' came from the honesty and integrity of my great-grandfather McCoy, who was once nominated for governor."

Dr. Quicksolve almost choked on his coffee. He sat next to

Junior, who smiled and winked knowingly. Captain Reelumin, Lieutenant Rootumout, and Fred Fraudstop listened attentively. Fred was hoping for the chance to talk about his ancestors. His chances were slim. Blowhard seemed to have an endless supply of air and continued talking without the usual necessity of taking a breath.

"Why don't you tell him, Dad?" Junior whispered to Dr. Quicksolve.

What does Junior think Dr. Quicksolve should say?

Answer on page 91

Ben Again

• • • • • • • • •

It was Benjamin Clayborn Blowhard's last night in town. He would be off to "the East" in the morning. For "government reasons" he could not say exactly where he was going. Also "for government reasons" he could not say what he did for the government.

Sergeant Rebekah Shurshot had invited Blowhard and Dr. Quicksolve out to dinner. Dr. Quicksolve reluctantly accepted, to avoid hurting her feelings. As they listened to the end of another of Blowhard's stories, Rebekah said, "You certainly are a man of adventure."

"I come by it honestly," Blowhard replied. Dr. Quicksolve cringed at the thought of hearing more about Blowhard's forefathers. "My ancestors were rugged individuals. My great-great-grandfather was a sheriff back in the late 1800s. One story my father used to tell about him was when he was almost killed standing over his mother's grave. He was alone at the small cemetery. He took off his hat and held it reverently over his heart. That is what saved him. A bullet, fired by a vengeful desperado my great-great-grandfather had arrested for murder years before, slammed into his wristwatch. His wrist was bruised badly, but the watch saved his life.

"He drew his Colt 45s and shot the gun out of

the bad guy's hand. They both mounted their horses, and the chase began. Great-great-grandfather caught up with the killer and dove out of his saddle, bringing the man down off his horse and to the ground. The fistfight lasted 20 minutes before that outlaw gave up because he just could not swing his arms any more. Both his eyes were so swollen from receiving punches that he could not see what he was swinging at!"

Dr. Quicksolve excused himself from the table to avoid laughing out loud.

What was wrong with Ben Blowhard's story this time?

Answer on page 93.

Jokers Wild

• • • • • • • • •

The snowing had just begun, but the bitter winter wind forced Dr. J.L. Quicksolve to grab his hat with one hand and hold his collar closed with the other as he got out of his VW Beetle and walked past the ice-frosted car in the driveway. He walked carefully up the icy steps to the door of the house.

Miss Forkton opened the door when he rang the bell. He introduced himself, and she invited him in. "It sure is cold out there," he said.

"Too cold for burglars, you would think," came her reply.

"Tell me about your robbery, Miss Forkton," Dr. Quicksolve said as he took off his coat. Miss Forkton took his coat and laid it on top of her own fur coat on a chair next to the phone table.

"Well, I just got home a few minutes ago. When I came in the door and saw my safe open," she said, pointing to an open wall safe, "I went straight to the phone and called you. I am glad you could get here so fast."

"Yes, we may have a hot trail for such a cold night," Quicksolve mused.

"I had a fortune in jewels stolen, Dr. Quicksolve. I don't think this is a good time for jokes!" she said.

"I agree with you one hundred percent. So why

did you bring me out on such a cold night for this joke of yours, Miss Forkton?" the detective asked.

Why did he mistrust Miss Forkton?

Answer on page 95.

Threat

• • • • • • • • •

It was not the first time Dr. J.L. Quicksolve had received a threatening letter. This one, though, seemed a little more menacing than the usual prank. It contained a small piece of plastic that was a bit of casing from a cylinder of dynamite.

Dr. Quicksolve had taken steps to protect himself. He left his VW Beetle parked on the street as a temptation for the would-be bomber. He set up a video camera in his upstairs window to watch his car through the night and keep a taped record.

Others were watching too. Sergeant Rebekah

Shurshot drove the unmarked police car through the dark neighborhood. Officer Longarm sat beside her. They were going to drive by Dr. Quicksolve's house "just to see if anything looked suspicious." They knew about the threat and were worried about their friend.

As they drove closer to the house, they saw a large sedan about half a block behind Dr. Quicksolve's VW. The car was dark. They did not realize it was occupied by two men until they were beside it. The small flame of a lighter flickered up to a cigarette on the passenger's side.

"Let's check this out," Sergeant Shurshot said, pulling up in front of the parked car.

She approached the driver's door. Officer Longarm went around to the other side. The driver's window came down. The smiling, mustached driver spoke. "Hi. We're lost, and we stopped to look at our map," he said, holding a map up to prove his point. "Could you help us out?"

Sergeant Shurshot was not smiling when she said, "Please get out of the car slowly with your hands up."

The two men looked at the officers and their drawn guns and did what they were told.

What tipped off the officers?

Answer on page 91.

Plunger and Snake

● ● ● ● ● ● ● ● ●

Dr. J.L. Quicksolve got out of his car. He pulled
his hat down tighter on his head to avoid losing it
to the icy wind on another snowy winter morning.
He walked between the two police cars to the
front door of Plunger and Snake's Plumbing Sup-
plies. He pulled the front door open and walked
in.

Lieutenant Rootumout was talking with a man
who played with his mustache nervously as he
spoke. Another officer was kneeling over a body

on the floor. Lieutenant Rootumout looked up at Dr. Quicksolve and introduced him to Paul Plunger, the mustached man. Indicating the body, Lieutenant Rootumout said, "Stan Snake."

Dr. Quicksolve sat down and listened to Plunger's story. Plunger paused and rolled up his shirt sleeves. "Yes," he said, "I saw Stan's body when I came in this morning, but I did not have time to do anything. Someone had been hiding behind the door and stuck a gun in my back. He made me lie facedown on the floor. Then he left."

"Did he take anything?" Lieutenant Rootumout asked.

"I don't know. We don't keep any money here overnight, if that is what you mean. Maybe that is why he killed Stan—because he could not give him any money. The killer would not know our secretary, Miss Supplewrist, takes the day's earnings to the bank after we close. She brings money for petty cash when she comes to work every morning. She has not come in yet today," Mr. Plunger explained, giving his mustache a final tug.

"We'll talk to her when she arrives," Lieutenant Rootumout said.

"We'll ask if she has any idea why you killed your partner," Dr. Quicksolve added.

Why did Dr. Quicksolve suspect Plunger killed Snake?

Answer on page 94.

Shortstop's Bike

• • • • • • • • •

Junior got off his bike and knocked on his friend Shortstop's front door. Shortstop was usually sitting on his bike in the driveway when Junior came by, and they would ride to school together each morning. "Where's your bike?" Junior asked when Shortstop came to the door with his backpack in his hand and a sad look on his face.

"Somebody stole it from our garage yesterday afternoon," Shortstop said.

"Did you see anything?" Junior asked.

"No," Shortstop answered, "but my sister did. She heard a noise and looked out the window just in time to see a kid riding off on my bike. She doesn't know who it was, though. She only saw his back. She said he had on a denim jacket. It could have been anyone."

"We can check the bikes at school," Junior said as he pushed his bike down the sidewalk beside Shortstop.

Prissy Powers, the cutest girl on the cheerleading squad, was standing by the long row of bikes behind the school. "Hi, Junior. Hi, Shortstop. How come you're walking?"

"My bike was stolen yesterday," Shortstop said.

"I think we'll find it," Junior said confidently as he walked down the long row of bikes, stroking the crossbar of the first one of many that looked like Shortstop's.

"But there are so many that are just alike, even yours," Prissy said to Junior.

"That's good," Junior said, moving down the row to the next bike like Shortstop's.

Why does Junior think it is good that so many bikes look alike? What is he doing?

Answer on page 90.

Claude Viciously

• • • • • • • •

"The ringmaster insisted Claude Viciously use that new lion in his act because he was so big and aggressive—a crowd pleaser," Mrs. Viciously told Dr. J.L. Quicksolve as they sat in her trailer discussing her husband's death. "The lion wasn't trained. Claude was afraid of him. Claude hadn't been afraid in years, but this scared him. He sat right there, barely two hours ago at breakfast, and decided he wouldn't go in with the new lion unless he had his gun loaded. He was always proud that he could work with the big cats without even the blank pistol some trainers use. He was scared. Animals sense that, you know."

Claude's body lay in the center of the ring covered by a blanket. The lion had been put away, and Lieutenant Rootumout and two other men stood beside the body. One man, obviously the ringmaster, wore a fancy suit with long tails. The other, a performer, wore black tights and a bright red sash.

"I should not have insisted he use that new lion," the ringmaster said, clearly shaken by the death.

Lieutenant Rootumout held up a clear plastic bag as Dr. Quicksolve approached. It contained a large revolver. "It's empty," he said to Dr. Quicksolve.

"I can't believe he forgot the bullets," Stretch

Prettitight said. "He was afraid of that lion."

Dr. Quicksolve bent down and lifted the edge of the blanket to look at the body. "Looks like murder," he said.

"Lions can't be charged with murder," Stretch scoffed.

"*You* can," Dr. Quicksolve replied.

Why does Dr. Quicksolve suspect Stretch?

Answer on page 91.

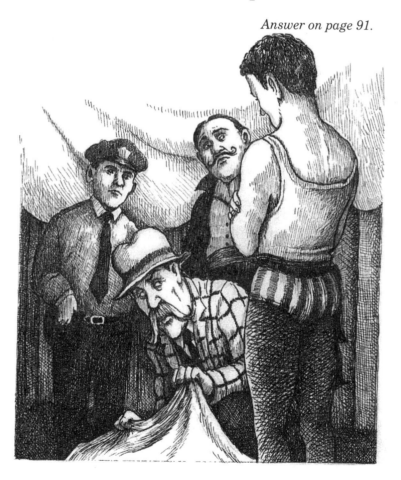

Dedingon

• • • • • • • • •

"He's Dedingon—apparently stabbed," Sergeant Rebekah Shurshot said to Dr. J.L. Quicksolve as they stood on the freshly shoveled sidewalk looking down at the lifeless and quickly freezing body lying in the snow. Police officers moved around them. One was taking pictures. Others were searching the area. Tracking dogs were being unloaded from a police station wagon. "A neighbor was found walking away from the body. He's a suspect. The neighbor and Dedingon had been feuding for years. Dedingon phoned the police station just a week ago and said his neighbor had threatened him."

"Let's talk to the neighbor," Dr. Quicksolve said.

Mrs. Trusted met them at the door. They stamped the snow from their feet, and she took their coats. A pair of men's boots and wet gloves lay on the floor by the door.

"Your husband...?" Dr. Quicksolve started to ask.

"They took Notubi to the police station. I hope they don't think he did it," Mrs. Trusted said.

"Was he out for a walk early this morning?" Sergeant Shurshot asked.

"Yes," she answered. "He likes to walk in the snow. They don't have snow in his country. He especially likes to walk in the morning before day-light."

"Apparently, Mr. Dedingon enjoyed early morning walks too," Dr. Quicksolve said.

A police officer walked up to Dr. Quicksolve and Sergeant Shurshot as they left the house. "The dogs haven't been able to pick up a trail, and no one has found a weapon," he told them.

"Although the snow makes it difficult, the fact the dogs can't pick up a scent makes me suspect Notubi. On the other hand, caught at the scene, he didn't have time to get rid of the weapon," Sergeant Shurshot said.

"Maybe Dedingon helped him get rid of the evidence," Dr. Quicksolve said.

What could Dr. Quicksolve mean?

Answer on page 92.

Unwanted Attention

● ● ● ● ● ● ● ●

"Lucy Looker is being stalked," Sergeant Rebekah Shurshot announced as Dr. J.L. Quicksolve handed her a cup of coffee.

"The movie star," he said.

"Yes. This note was found under her windshield wiper this morning," Sergeant Shurshot said. She handed him a red heart-shaped piece of construction paper. The edges were jagged and wrinkled, as if cut by a young child. The smeared print was in blue ink. "Be my valentine or hearts will be broken," it said. It was unsigned.

"This is the third note with a veiled threat," Sergeant Shurshot explained. "Lucy Looker has been getting phone calls too. The caller doesn't say anything, just listens."

"Have you been able to trace the calls?" Dr. Quicksolve asked.

"Yes, we have. They come from an apartment where two young college men live," Sergeant Shurshot said.

"Then you have your suspects," said Dr. Quicksolve.

"I don't think they're in it together. They could easily alibi for each other, but they don't. Each one said the other was alone in the apartment when the calls were made. We can't tell who it was from what they tell us. It looks as if one was going out and the other coming in about the time of each call. It could be either of them. I hope our handwriting expert will be able to tell us which one wrote the note."

"I don't think we'll need an expert to figure that out," Dr. Quicksolve said, "but, of course, an expert can verify our conclusion."

How did Dr. Quicksolve think he could tell who wrote the note?

Answer on page 90.

The Mings' Things

• • • • • • • • •

As they walked around the house, Officer Longarm told Dr. J.L. Quicksolve about the robbery.

"Mary Ming said she often forgets to lock her back door. She said her neighborhood has had very little crime for years and Inky, her cocker spaniel, would at least bark at a stranger and scare him away. She went to bed late last night, though, and she woke up and found her two antique vases, handed down from her husband's ancestors, were missing. She said they were valuable and very important to her family. There are no signs of forced entry, and nothing else is missing."

Dr. Quicksolve and Officer Longarm went into the kitchen, where Marvin and Mary Ming sat sipping coffee. Their friend Jade Greene was consoling Mary. "No one is going to break anything so valuable," she said, "and the police will find..."

"Find what?" said a petite red-haired woman who had just come in through the back door. "I saw the police car. What happened?"

Officer Longarm and Dr. Quicksolve looked questioningly at the new arrival. "This is Donna, my neighbor," Mary Ming said.

Looking through the short hallway at the empty end of the mantel, Donna cried, "Your vase! Oh, no! Did you have a burglar?" she asked.

"Yes," Mary Ming replied sadly. "We did."

"The police will take care of things," Jade Greene said, continuing to console her friend.

"I am sure they will find them," Donna added, supporting Jade's confidence. You will get them back."

"Don't worry, dear," Marvin Ming told his wife, and put his hand on hers.

"Thanks for your confidence," Officer Longarm said.

"Were you green with envy or just greedy?" Dr. Quicksolve asked.

Who was Dr. Quicksolve talking to? Why?

Answer on page 92.

Captain Maxwell Marchwell

•••••••••

It was a cold March day, but Dr. J.L. Quicksolve sat in a cozy little coffee shop across from the university campus. He was totally aware of his surroundings, noticing who came in, who went out, who wore what, and even what they ordered. At the same time he listened intently as he looked into the green eyes of the young lawyer sitting across the small table from him. She stopped occasionally to sip her cappuccino. Her name was Gladys Notmie, and she was concerned about a client.

"Not only has she just lost her father, but her cousin is trying to take her inheritance," she told Dr. Quicksolve. "Her father was a proud soldier. He just made captain and retired this year."

"Tell me about her father's accident," Dr. Quicksolve said.

"His car fell on him," she said rather bluntly. "He was under the car making repairs or looking at something. They never did find anything wrong with the car. There was nothing wrong with the jack. The police think he might have accidentally kicked it or something. Anyway, he was found dead under his car in the garage."

"And the inheritance?" the detective asked.

Gladys took a letter out of her briefcase. "My client's cousin claims this letter was written by Captain Marchwell and she gets all the inheritance." She read the letter, which was short and to the point: "May 2, 1995. I, Captain Maxwell Marchwell, hereby request that all my money and possessions be given to my late sister's daughter, Ima Scoundrel, upon my death. Signed, Captain Maxwell Marchwell."

"Interesting," Dr. Quicksolve responded.

"What can we do? This whole thing looks very suspicious to me," Gladys said.

"I think your client has nothing to worry about," said Dr. Quicksolve.

What has Dr. Quicksolve noticed?

Answer on page 93.

Flora and Fauna

• • • • • • • • •

Junior had two cute little cousins named Flora and Fauna. They were a year younger than Junior. They were also identical twins. Almost no one could distinguish one from the other—especially when they didn't want to be distinguished!

Added to the confusion of their phenomenal resemblance was the fact that they were distant cousins of Junior's in more ways than one. Junior had only seen them once before. So he had the cards stacked against him when it came to sorting out who was who.

He had heard how much Flora and Fauna enjoyed confounding people and playing "twin games." He also knew it would be fun to see them again at Grandma and Grandpa Quicksolve's farm, and he looked forward to the challenge.

Grandma's Pancakes

● ● ● ● ● ● ● ●

Grandma and Grandpa Quicksolve met Junior at the train station early in the morning. He tossed his bag into the back of Grandma's pickup, and the three of them headed for the farm. "Wait till you see your cousins," Grandma told Junior.

When they entered through the back door and into the kitchen, Grandma was surprised to see a plate on the table covered with pancake syrup. A fork, also covered with syrup, looked stuck to the table beside a wadded napkin. An empty box of frozen waffles sat on the counter. Someone had eaten breakfast. Grandma was a little upset. "I told those girls I would cook pancakes for everybody when we got back."

"Maybe a burglar broke in and made himself breakfast," Grandpa said.

Grandma called the twins downstairs and introduced them to their cousin, Junior, whom they had not seen for years. Junior tried to find some way to tell the two girls apart as they stood there in their bib-overall shorts and held out their hands to shake his. They looked just alike, except one had her left hand in her pocket and the other had her left hand on her hip.

"Who had breakfast?" Grandma asked. "We were going to eat pancakes together."

The girls smiled sheepishly and looked at each other. Junior remembered that when they were younger they would blame each other for things. Apparently, they had decided that things would work out better if they just kept quiet.

"Maybe we should weigh them," Grandpa suggested.

"I can tell you who did it, Grandma, if it really matters," Junior said.

"Never mind," said Grandma. "You can help me cook, and they can both do the dishes."

How did Junior know who had eaten?

Answer on page 94.

License Nonsense

• • • • • • • • •

Flora and Fauna were a little frustrated at how easily their cousin Junior figured out which of them had eaten the early breakfast. At the same time they admired his cleverness. Maybe he was more closely related to them than they thought.

The twins sat in the back seat of Grandpa Quicksolve's car on their way to Kris Crossing, and Junior sat in the front next to Grandpa. The sisters whispered to each other and decided to give Junior a test.

"I like to look at license plates," Flora said.

"There's one that says MY TOY," said Fauna, pointing to a bright-red sportscar racing past them.

"Look at the van in front of us," Grandpa said. Its license says MOMS BUS."

"I like those special ones," Flora said, "with words."

"It seems funny to me," Grandpa said, "when you see one with a name and then a number, like BOB-3. It makes me wonder what happened to BOB-1 and BOB-2."

"Maybe it's a woman who married a lot of men named Bob," Junior joked.

"Regular licenses have letters and numbers. I wonder why they use letters," Flora said.

"Maybe they're easier to remember," Fauna replied.

"I guess if they use both, they can make more license plates," Junior said.

"Do you suppose they could make more plates if they just used numbers than if they just used letters?" Flora asked, directing her question to Junior.

"That's an easy question," Junior answered.

But is the answer easy?

Answer on page 93.

120 Hippopotamuses

• • • • • • • •

Grandpa parked in front of Joe's Barbershop on Main Street across from an alley. Junior and his twin cousins got out of the car. Junior didn't know Flora and Fauna were setting him up. They wanted to see if he was smart enough to be considered one of the family.

Junior was startled for a second when he saw a young girl standing in front of the barbershop wearing bib-overall shorts and a white tee-shirt that matched the outfits the twins wore.

"Hi, Bobbi," Fauna said. "Grandpa and our cousin Junior are getting haircuts. Why don't we walk down the street and get some ice cream?"

"You three look like you're on a team," Grandpa said, unwittingly falling into stride with the girls.

"We do like to run together," Bobbi said.

"Are you good runners?" Junior asked.

"Fauna is the fastest girl in the world," Flora said. "She can run around that block in two minutes!"

Junior looked up and down the street, making his own estimations. "That's hard to believe," he said.

"Bet you an ice cream," Flora said.

"Okay," Junior agreed.

"You start counting hippopotamuses when she starts running. Fauna will be back here before you can count 120 hippopotamuses. Bobbi and I will go up the alley and make sure she doesn't cheat. We can do it while you're getting a haircut. You can watch from the barbershop," Flora said.

"I think I read a story like this once," Junior said.

Flora looked worried for a second. "Was it *Chariots of Fire*?" she asked.

"I don't think so," Junior answered, "but I'm going to enjoy the free ice cream."

What has Junior figured out?

Answer on page 91.

Car Caper

• • • • • • • • •

Dr. J.L. Quicksolve watched from Sergeant Rebekah Shurshot's office as a tough-looking, gum-chewing teenager was led into the interrogation room for questioning. His name was Joey Rider. He had been brought in for car theft. The car had been stolen from a used-car lot. The single key had been left in the ignition for just a few minutes. The salesman turned his back for a moment, and someone had jumped into the car and sped away. The police were called immediately.

They chased the car until it rounded a corner and disappeared down a dead-end alley. Joey was found alone in the alley, but he had not actually been seen driving the car. The car was there, and the key was missing. Both Joey and the alley were searched. No key was found.

Dr. Quicksolve came in to start the questioning. Joey was sitting alone at the table. "Can I have a cigarette?" Joey asked.

"Aren't you a little young to smoke?" Sergeant Shurshot asked.

"How about a stick of gum then? My mouth is a little dry," Joey said.

"I think we can turn the tables on this young man and find that missing key, the evidence we need to solve this sticky problem," Dr. Quicksolve said wryly.

What did Dr. Quicksolve do next?

Answer on page 91.

Tubbs-Tibbs

•••••••••

The stolen jewelry had turned up at a pawnshop. The owner, Ike Tradit, remembered getting it from a tall man with brown hair and a mustache. Two suspects were found, and both of them fit the description. The pawnbroker couldn't say for certain which was the jewel thief. He said the two men looked a lot alike, and both had been in the shop. He was sure it was one of the two, but he wasn't sure which one. Adding to the confusion was the similarity of their names—Tim Tubbs and Tom Tibbs.

Dr. J.L. Quicksolve questioned both men. Tim Tubbs was first. Dr. Quicksolve showed him the jewelry. "Have you ever seen this before?" he asked Tubbs.

"No. I don't know what you're holding me for. I didn't steal that stuff or anything else," Tim said.

"It was stolen. You're right about that," Dr. Quicksolve said, "and it was pawned at Ike Tradit's shop. You go there a lot, don't you?"

"Yeah, I go there, but I didn't take that jewelry. I told you, I never saw it before."

Then the detective talked with the second suspect, Tom Tibbs. He showed Tibbs the jewelry and asked if he had ever seen it before.

"No, I have never seen it, and I did not steal it. Talk to Tim Tubbs. Ike gets us mixed up a lot," Tibbs replied.

"But you do take things to Ike Tradit's pawnshop, right?" Dr. Quicksolve asked .

"Sometimes I have, but nothing that's been stolen," Tibbs said.

"I don't think that is true, Mr. Tibbs," Dr. Quicksolve said.

Why did Dr. Quicksolve suspect Tibbs?

Answer on page 94.

Diamond Run

• • • • • • • • •

Welles Fargoh, a security guard, was telling Dr. J.L. Quicksolve what had happened. "I was delivering a satchel full of diamonds for a jewelry store. I had just stopped at a light when two riders on a motorcycle pulled up on the right side of my car. I glanced at them. Nothing seemed unusual. I was looking up at the light when I heard a crash beside me. I was pelted with flying glass. Apparently, the passenger on the motorcycle had smashed my window with a crowbar or something.

"Before I could react, he reached his arm into my car through the broken window and grabbed the satchel. He hopped back on the motorcycle, and they sped off. I called the police on my car phone and told them what happened, but they haven't caught anyone yet, as far as I know," Fargoh explained.

"Can you describe the men, Mr. Fargoh?" Dr. Quicksolve asked.

"Sure, the driver was tall with short curly brown hair. The other guy was shorter. I think he had a mustache."

"And the motorcycle?" Quicksolve asked.

"It was bright red, matching their helmets. I'm not sure what kind it was," said Fargoh. "They drove away so quickly and turned down an alley. The guy on the back almost fell off when they turned."

"I think the only thing you're sure about is what really happened to those diamonds. Why don't you tell me?"

Why did Dr. Quicksolve think Fargoh knew what happened to the diamonds?

Answer on page 89.

Stolen Sportscar

• • • • • • • • •

Dr. J.L. Quicksolve answered the phone. It was Peter Pompous. His sportscar had been stolen. Dr. Quicksolve said he would be right over.

Dr. Quicksolve liked his VW, a restored Beetle. It was fun without being flashy. And unlike

Peter's fancy sportscar, it didn't tend to attract thieves or carjackers.

When Dr. Quicksolve arrived, Peter let him in. "Tell me what you know about this," Dr. Quicksolve said.

"I'd just gotten back from the office. I got out of my sportscar when somebody hit me over the head. He took my keys and stole my car," Pompous explained.

"Did you see who hit you?" asked Dr. Quicksolve.

"No. It was dark and rainy. I had my head down and he came up from behind me. I was surprised. I didn't know what hit me."

"What did you do when you got up?"

"Well, the guy was gone, so I didn't see him. I don't know what he looked like. I went into the house and called you right away," Pompous said.

"Was anyone in the house who might have seen your assailant?" Dr. Quicksolve asked.

"No. I live alone. The cleaning lady comes in on Monday and Friday. The house was empty. I'm sure glad I had that car insured!" Pompous said.

"I'm afraid you may not be able to collect on that insurance, Peter. There are some flaws in your story," Dr. Quicksolve stated confidently.

Why did Dr. Quicksolve doubt Peter's story?

Answer on page 92.

Answers

•••••••••

Murder Between Friends (page 6)—Dr. Quicksolve suspected Tweeter. Her hearing seemed fine and her music was not loud enough to drown out the sound of gunshots. The hall was quiet and the music did not interfere with their conversation. She may have been angry with Terry for complaining about her music.

Many hearing-impaired people would be able to hear gunshots. Miss Blossom's Labrador was apparently a "hearing ear dog" who brought her to the door when Dr. Quicksolve knocked quietly. There is no reason to suspect Miss Blossom.

Telephone Ring (page 22)—He expected to see a phone or credit card number on the pad that would match the number belonging to the man in the jacket. Dr. Quicksolve knew that thieves stand around open phones to listen while people say their card numbers into the phone. Then these criminals use the numbers to make calls or charge things. This time, the crook did not get away.

Thanksgiving Blessing (page 32)—Dr. Quicksolve knows Thanksgiving Day is traditionally celebrated on the fourth Thursday of November, but in 1939 President Franklin D. Roosevelt set it one week earlier to help business by adding one more week of shopping between Thanksgiving and Christmas. After 1941, Congress changed Thanksgiving back to the fourth Thursday of November.

Diamond Run (page 85)—Fargoh gave descriptions of the thieves that included the length and hair color, which he could not have seen if they were wearing motorcycle helmets.

Ben Boinkt (page 24)—Dr. Quicksolve doubts their story and wonders if Mr. Boinkt was hit at all. How could the robbers find the safe, open it, and be gone so quickly if Mr. and Mrs. Boinkt were both unconscious? He thinks Ben Boinkt and Glenda Cheatenhart killed Mrs. Boinkt.

Inheritance (page 8)—Dr. Quicksolve wanted to talk to the cousin from North Dakota because he had already eliminated the niece. The deceased, an only child and a bachelor, could not have a niece.

Drive-By Incident (page 42)—He said she hit his outstretched arm as she passed. Since we drive on the right side of the road, that would have been his left arm, but his right arm was in the sling.

Shortstop's Bike (page 62)—Because there are so many bikes that look alike, the thief would probably think it was safe to ride it to school, believing Shortstop could not identify his bike.

Junior and Shortstop had wisely etched their names inconspicuously under the crossbars of their bikes where no one would notice, but Junior could feel the engraving with his fingers.

Unwanted Attention (page 68)—The ink was smeared. This very often happens when a leftie writes with his hand twisted around above the writing. The jagged edge of the paper suggests left-handedness too, since most scissors are designed for righties and tend to be difficult for lefties to use. Dr. Quicksolve only has to see which roommate is left-handed.

Floating Above South Dakota (page 50)—Ben Blowhard talks about piloting a hot-air balloon hundreds of miles with exact precision when, in fact, a hot-air balloon cannot be steered. You can only control the ascent and descent.

Car Caper (page 81)—He turned the table over to show that the gum was holding the missing key to the bottom of the table. Dr. Quicksolve saw Joey chewing gum when he came in, yet he asked for a cigarette and gum a few minutes later. Quicksolve knew Joey had done something with the gum in his mouth and suspected he probably hid the key while he was searched earlier.

Quicksolve, the Movie (page 10)—The driver said he had just gotten there, yet he was parked near the theater entrance when the lot was full and cars lined the street. He would have had to arrive early to get such a good parking space.

The Real McCoy (page 52)—Junior knew Blowhard's story about "the real McCoy" was not true. It is generally accepted that the expression is connected to an invention that automatically lubricates moving parts on many kinds of machines. The inventor was an African-American named Elijah McCoy.

Claude Viciously (page 64)—Being a circus performer, Stretch would have known lion tamers use blanks, yet he said "bullets." He only could have known there had been bullets in the gun if he was the one who took them out.

120 Hippopotamuses (page 79)—Junior thinks Fauna will start the race while Flora and Bobbi wait at the other end of the alley. Even before Fauna has had enough time to round the corner out of sight, Flora will start running the second half of the race. After Flora finishes the race, Fauna will come down the alley with Bobbi, and they will say it was a fair race.

Threat (page 58)—The driver said they were looking at a map, yet he had not turned on the interior light to read it.

Capture (page 35)—Dr. Quicksolve knew that the Mysterious Woman, a master of disguises, was as tall as Fred at the last party when she was all dressed up including high heels, which would have made her a little taller than she really was. The woman in the room was taller than Fred, so she couldn't be the suspect. The "man," however, without high heels, was the only one in the room who was the right height. She had changed into some of Fred's clothes and hid her purse when she realized she couldn't escape through the window.

Shattered Crystal (page 12)—The front door faces east. Remember, Dr. Quicksolve felt the east wind at his back as he faced the door. In the late afternoon, the sun could not have cast a shadow into the house from the front door.

Stolen Sportscar (page 87)—Peter said the thief took his keys, but then he went right into the empty house, which surely would have been locked.

The Ming's Things (page 70)—Dr. Quicksolve was not talking to Jade Greene. He was talking to Donna, because she said, "You will get them back," when she could only have known one vase was missing by looking down the hallway at the empty end of the mantel.

Motorcycle Getaway (page 20)—Dr. Quicksolve did not believe the clerk's story. How could a man clutching a money box to his chest and carrying a gun jump on a motorcycle and drive away so quickly? Even if the engine were running, the motorcyclist would have needed both hands free to work the clutch and gas.

Dedingon (page 66)—Notubi, fascinated by the winter weather, may have used a sharp icicle to stab Dedingon, whose warm body could have melted the evidence even as he lay dying.

Professor Wright (page 14)—Dr. Quicksolve knew, as Professor Wright confirmed when he came out of the coma, that he would not have written, "If I were him." He would have written, "If I were he."

Ben Again (page 54)—The fancy shooting and the long fistfight between the two men is hard to believe. The real problem with the story, though, is the wristwatch. There were wristwatches in the late 1800s, but they were designed only for women! Men used pocket watches at that time.

License Nonsense (page 77)—The girls think they can fool Junior because everyone knows there are more numbers than letters. But it's necessary to consider the number of combinations possible in the limited space available on a license plate using numbers compared to the number of combinations using letters. Since there are only 10 individual numerals (0–9) and 26 letters (A–Z), you can make more license plates with letters than numbers.

Socks (page 26)—Bobby said they were playing a team from Jackson. That means his was the home team, which would bat second and wouldn't bat the last inning if they were ahead after the visitors' last bat.

Shadow Heart Trail (page 30)—The voice on the walkie-talkie said they were two and a half miles down the trail and they turned toward the morning sun. They must have turned right toward the east and the morning sun.

Captain Maxwell Marchwell (page 72)—Since Captain Marchwell was made captain and then retired in March, he would not have signed a letter "Captain Maxwell Marchwell" the previous May. It must be a forgery.

Buz (page 28)—Buz's story about catching bees was his alibi for being out in the field with the jar. He doesn't really know very much about bees. He made the common mistake of calling the large black-and-yellow bumblebee a yellow jacket, even though it is actually not a bee but a small wasp.

Strikeout (page 16)—Junior thinks Homer should not be trusted because he sells counterfeit baseball cards. Mickey Mantle played for the Yankees in 1951, so there cannot be a 1953 rookie card.

Fakeout (page 40)—The fact the driver has no identification is very suspicious. It could be the robber and/or Spider himself. Dr. Quicksolve suspected the robber pulled over to look as if he had fixed a flat and had been there a longer time. He could easily and quickly have let the air out of the spare tire to make it flat. If it had just been taken off the car on this snowy morning, however, it would also be wet.

Grandma's Pancakes (page 75)—Junior had shaken each girl's hand. One was still sticky from the syrup on the fork.

Tubbs-Tibbs (page 83)—Tibbs knew the stolen jewelry was taken to Tradit's Pawnshop.

Thurston Drinker (page 44)—Thurston Drinker claimed he was tied up in the woods for days, yet he has a narrow mustache instead of a full beard.

Plunger and Snake (page 60)—Plunger said someone hid behind the door. Dr. Quicksolve had just pulled the door open to come in. If the door pulled out to open, no one could have been hiding behind it on the inside.

Final Payoff (page 38)—She said he was upset about a letter he received that day. Since Thanksgiving Day is a national holiday, mail would not be delivered.

Coddled Coed (page 18)—Sergeant Shurshot believes Holly took the money. She thinks Holly made up a quick alibi because no one with a cat in the house would leave unwrapped fish on the counter.

Australian Adventure (page 48)—The story is hard to believe even if you don't know that Australia has no ferocious wild bears.

Jokers Wild (page 56)—Miss Forkton said she had just arrived home, yet her car was frosted over.

Index

•••••••••